THE ERA OF RAIL BLUE

MARK JAMIESON

AMBERLEY

Acknowledgements

My thanks to Roger Smith, Tony Callaghan, John Dedman, Nigel Nicholls, Pete Nurse and Steve McMullin for their help, assistance or contributions with this book. I must also pass on my thanks to the various internet sites that have proved invaluable in researching some of the images used, particularly the likes of Six Bells Junction, Derby Sulzers, Rail Gen Archive and Paul Appleby's Class 47 site.

Finally, I must give a very special mention to Nic Joynson for his involvement in this book; I couldn't have done it without you. Thank you.

Front cover: Large-logo No. 37264 passes Hawkeridge Junction, on the approach to Westbury on 12 June 1991, working 8A01, the 07.01 Gloucester New Yard–Westbury Yard. (Steve McMullin) (Author's Collection)

Rear cover: Passing the attractive Great Western Type 7D signal box at Malvern Wells, opened in 1919, is this Tyseley-based DMU operating 2V38, the 16.32 Birmingham New Street–Hereford, on 23 June 1989. (Steve McMullin)

First published 2022

Amberley Publishing
The Hill, Stroud
Gloucestershire, GL5 4EP

www.amberley-books.com

Copyright © Mark Jamieson, 2022

The right of Mark Jamieson to be identified as the Author of this work has been asserted in accordance with the Copyrights, Designs and Patents Act 1988.

ISBN 978 1 4456 9772 7 (print)
ISBN 978 1 4456 9773 4 (ebook)

British Library Cataloguing in Publication Data. A catalogue record for this book is available from the British Library.

Origination by Amberley Publishing.
Printed in the UK.

Introduction

In railway history the 1960s will be remembered for mass line closures and the end of steam traction. Yet, these aspects were part of a wider agenda of evolution and modernisation of British Railways.

In 1964 British Railways produced a booklet highlighting some of these plans. Called *British Railways project xp64 – eXpress Passenger*, it described a new travelling experience: 'The design of the prototype British Railways xp64 passenger coaches represents a completely new approach to rail travel comfort and amenity. Within the practical restrictions of length, width, height and other basic dimensions, a large number of new ideas have been introduced.' British Railways rebranded itself and in 1965 became British Rail, introducing a standard corporate identity and with it a new livery. The era of rail blue had begun. This new branding would see the multitude of steam-age regional liveries replaced by Monastral blue, with yellow front ends to locomotives and multiple units, and passenger coaching stock finished in Monastral blue and grey. Perhaps one of the most striking changes would be the new double arrow logo, which has become an iconic symbol of British Rail, and continues to be associated with Britain's railway to this day.

Stations, uniforms, paperwork, signage and existing rolling stock began to adopt the new livery and identity. British Rail also introduced a new generation of locomotives, multiple units and rolling stock, and from 1965 carried the new corporate livery from new. For the following twenty years or so, trains carried this new livery operating nationwide, and until 1977 British Rail applied the livery rigidly, without exception. Minor deviations from the standard livery began in 1977 with Stratford depot's silver-grey roof for their Class 47s. Another example was the application of white window surrounds to the cabs of Finsbury Park's Class 55s during 1979. But in 1978 British Rail unveiled the first major revision to the livery. Stratford Works released No. 56036 in what would become known as the 'large logo' locomotive livery. This bold development of the standard BR blue featured a full-height version of the iconic BR double arrow logo. The new livery extended the safety yellow front end to cover the cabs of the locomotives and large bodyside numerals, creating an eye-catching design feature. This livery variation was to become one of the most popular liveries of the post-steam age.

History now records that the rail blue era lasted from the mid-1960s through to the early 1990s, although many enthusiasts in those early days struggled to accept change following the end of steam, often dismissing it as boring. In the history of Britain's railways the rail blue era lasted for a short period of time, though it is now looked upon by those growing up at the time with great affection. This book is a celebration of that time, with many of the images appearing in print for the first time.

The author, and his contributors, have acquired some images used in *The Era of Rail Blue*, and such images appear here in good faith. Please contact the publisher if you believe an image has been included in error, and we will make the necessary changes at the first available opportunity.

An everyday sight from 1969. Brush Type 4 No. 1612 has just passed Twyford and is now approaching Sonning cutting while working a Paddington to Bristol service. On that cold crisp sunny lunchtime a procession of diesel hydraulic locomotives would have passed this location, and chances are the photographer may have been hoping for something like a Western, and may have been disappointed by 'just another Brush Type 4'. (Nic Joynson Collection)

No. D855 *Triumph* speeds away from Twyford on a blazing day in the summer of 1963 while working the 10.45 Paddington to Weston-Super-Mare service. No. D855 was less than two years old at the time, but the locomotive would last only a further eight years before it was withdrawn from service. Before the launch of rail blue, the trains of British Railways carried no single, consistent livery. This photograph illustrates a common, though not universal combination. The locomotive carries British Railways green, complete with a small yellow warning panel. The coaches are carrying the maroon livery introduced in 1956. Yet, this combination was by no means standardised in 1963. (Nic Joynson Collection)

The sixth class of AC locomotive type ordered by British Rail, the AL6. New to traffic from August 1965 the AL6, later to become Class 86 under TOPS classification, were turned out in a light shade of blue, known as electric blue, like all other AC locomotive types. With the decision already taken by the British Railways Board to go for Monastral blue, this electric blue livery would be short-lived. (Author's Collection)

Passing a colourful display of rosebay willowherb is this AL5 (later Class 85) in the attractive electric blue livery. British Rail standardised its colour scheme, and from 1965 rail blue, or Monastral blue, was the preferred colour. (Author Collection)

Where it all began for rail blue. The British Railways Board published a document in 1964 called *British Railways project xp64* – XP being an abbreviation for 'express passenger'. One of eight experimental coaches built during 1964, as part of the xp64 project, is M13407, seen here at Kings Cross on 13 June 1964 forming part of the 22.15 Kings Cross–Edinburgh. Brush Type 2 No. D5644 (TOPS number 31219) can be seen to the left, although its questionable if this was the actual train locomotive? (Roger Smith Collection)

A real museum piece by modern standards is this pre-nationalisation Gresley restaurant buffet coach E9132, which is seen at Cambridge on 30 April 1976 and already looking out of place among the Mk1 coaches either side of it. These teak body coaches, built at York in 1937 by the LNER, were finally phased out by 1977. (Roger Smith collection)

British Rail had introduced what was to become standard rail blue in 1965, but just thirteen years later a revised version was to appear: large logo. The first locomotive to appear in this new livery was No. 56036, which made its debut during August 1978 following its repaint at Stratford Works. What was to become an iconic livery was adopted for passenger locomotives, such as Class 37s, Class 47s, Class 50s and Class 73s. (Author's Collection)

A transitional scene at Kings Cross with remodelling and modernisation of the steam age infrastructure. There is a hive of activity going on with work on the track and signalling, yet all the while some services are still able to run from Platforms 7 to 11, with a Class 47 in Platform 8 and a Class 31 in Platform 10 and running over the newly relayed slow lines through Gasworks Tunnel. A Class 08 hauled spoil train is visible in Platform 3. To the left the southbound platform of Kings Cross York Road can be seen, with a single brake van on the platform line, which leads into the tunnel to Moorgate, known as the 'Widened Lines', which closed to passengers on 8 November 1976. (Author's Collection)

The train that revolutionised travel by rail in Britain during the 1970s: the High Speed Train, or Inter-City 125. This is Eastern Region set 254006, formed of power cars Nos 43064 and 43065, at Kings Cross station during September 1980. The first HST sets were introduced on British Rail's Western Region from 1976 and classified as Class 253, and on the Eastern and Scottish Region's from 1977 as Class 254. Both train sets were identical in appearance, the only difference being their formations, with the Eastern and Scottish Region sets generally having additional coaches. (George Marsh/Author's Collection)

A Class 47 storms past Cockwood heading west towards Dawlish Warren. Note the person fishing trackside to the right of the locomotive, but covering his face, as the train hurries by – blowing up dust as it passes at speed. This may have been an activity that would have been overlooked in the past, but not on today's modern railway. (Nigel Nicholls)

Originally introduced during the Second World War by the Southern Railway, and built at Eastleigh Works, was the 4-SUB unit. From 1946 a revised version of the original design was introduced with a new flat cab front. Surviving into the British Rail TOPS era, these 4-SUB units were designated Class 405, although they retained their pre-TOPS numbers. Viewed leaving Wimbledon on 16 March 1983 is a pair of these later design units, led by No. 4277, as they operate the 12.04 Waterloo to Shepperton service. These post-war suburban units were finally phased out by the Central Division of the Southern Region. The final revenue earning service operated by these type of electric units was on 6 September 1983. One unit, No. 4732, was eventually saved for preservation. (Tony Callaghan)

Sunday 30 May 1982 and No. 56066 with its train of HAA hoppers is stabled in Didcot Yard. The Class 56 was a heavy freight locomotives built between 1976 and 1984, this particular locomotive being new to traffic during December 1979. The build was divided between three locations with the first thirty locomotives built by Electoputere in Romania, which was a sub-contract to Brush of Loughborough. Nos 56031–56115 were constructed by BREL Doncaster, and the final twenty by BREL Crewe, with 56135 rolling off the production line in November 1984. (Tony Callaghan)

In fine weather Nos 26003, 47209 and 37085 are seen stabled on Millerhill on 25 March 1987. The Class 26 was scrapped during January 1995, while the Class 37 went onto become No. 37711, but would be scrapped during March 2006. However, No. 47209 survives as No. 57604 *Pendennis Castle*, and is something of a celebrity in its smart GWR green livery. (Nic Joynson)

This image was captured in one of the final years that the classic BR blue livery would be seen on the British Rail network, with sectorisation about to go into full swing, bringing with it a rainbow of different liveries. Seen here is a typical formation for such a working as No. 31456 is seen near Chinley, some 53 miles into a 77-mile journey, on 13 September 1987 working the 10.52 Liverpool to Sheffield service. (Nic Joynson)

London-bound No. 85018 approaches Bushey on Thursday 7 April 1983. It's still three months before the first Class 85 was withdrawn from traffic, when No. 85027 was taken out of service from July 1983. The class was withdrawn in its entirety by 1991. (John Dedman)

Promoted by the Severn Valley Railway Association, No. 40001 finds itself at the most unlikely destination of Weymouth on 21 May 1983, having worked 'The Wessex Whistler' railtour. Running from York, the Class 40 would come off at Westbury on the outward run in favour of Nos 33113 and 33118 for the run down from Westbury to Weymouth. Once the '40' had been refuelled at Westbury it would follow down light engine to Weymouth to pick up the return working. Here it is seen at Weymouth prior to departure back to York via Maiden Newton. (Author's Collection)

Single-line working between Bradford Junction and Westbury on 31 January 1988, and No. 47005 is on a loaded ballast train formed of ZFV Dogfish wagons, while coming 'wrong line' from Trowbridge is No.33057 – working 1O40, the 12.08 Bristol Temple Meads–Portsmouth Harbour, as it passes the worksite. (Steve McMullin)

The end of 'heritage' DMU operation on the Severn Beach branch, and the Bristol area generally. The final full day of DMU workings on the Severn Beach branch was Wednesday 23 September 1992, prior to the introduction of new Class 150 units. Here Class 116 DMU set No. C392 is captured at Redland station on that final day operating 2F10, the 12.55 Bristol Temple Meads–Severn Beach. (Steve McMullin)

Just five months left in traffic before its withdrawal in the November 1989, No. 50040 *Leviathan* works the 16.54 Bristol Temple Meads to Weymouth service on 16 June 1989, seen here arriving at Yeovil Pen Mill. (Nic Joynson)

On 20 July 1989, No. 47313 leads No. 37223, which is dead-in-tow, and heads north out of Westbury past Heywood village working 6V79, the 14.40 Salisbury Reception–Gloucester New Yard 'Speedlink' service. In the consist are PGA barrier wagons, Yeoman PTA and JYA wagons all going for repair, as well as various vans used for MoD traffic, and China clay tanks from Quidhampton. (Steve McMullin)

One of two Class 86s to receive a special livery celebrating the 150th anniversary of the 1829 Rainhill Trials in 1979. No. 86214 *Sans Pareil* and No. 86235 *Novelty* were chosen, and sported full yellow cabs and large bodyside numbers. The locos were named after locomotives that took part in the original trials, and were finished off with a full-height emblem marking the event. Here No. 86235 *Novelty* is seen at London Euston sporting this unique livery. (Author's Collection)

Tattenham Corner station, in Surrey, is the terminus of an 8-mile double-track branch from Purley, and the closest station to Epsom Downs Racecourse. The line and station opened on 4 June 1901, and third-rail electrification reached Tattenham Corner on 25 March 1928 with new electric passenger services commencing from that date. On to the BR blue era, and 4-SUB No. 4293 is pictured at Tattenham Corner station having just arrived from Charing Cross as a member of staff removes the paraffin tail lamp to place it on the other end for the 23-mile journey back to Charing Cross. (Roger Smith Collection)

A very cold morning at Leicester station on 21 February 1981 as No. 45144 *Royal Signals* arrives with a service from St Pancras. The Class 45s would soldier on along the Midland main line until Sunday 10 May 1987, which would be the final day of booked workings for the class in or out of the capital. (Author's Collection)

Ideal conditions at New Milton, between Brockenhurst and Bournemouth, fresh snow and crisp winter sunshine. Here No. 33116 propels a pair of 4-TC units towards New Milton station during January 1979. (John Dedman)

A cold and crisp day on the Settle & Carlisle as No. 40192 stands in the sidings at Ribblehead. Heavy withdrawals of the Class 40s were taking place during the 1980s, and No. 40192 would be taken out of traffic by January 1985, with final disposal quickly following a couple of months later at Doncaster Works. (Malcolm S. Trigg/Author's Collection)

The Edinburgh to Glasgow shuttle services during the 1970s had been operated by top-and-tail Class 27s on Mk2 stock, but British Rail identified a need to improve the service, not only with more modern stock and traction, but also with an increase in speed and frequency. And so, the Class 47/7 was created by converting a standard Class 47/4 with push-pull equipment and uprating its maximum speed from 95 mph to 100 mph. The improved service would incorporate Mk3 stock, and a new DBSO at the opposite end to the locomotive with which the train could be driven. The first of these trains were introduced from 1979 with an original fleet of twelve Class 47/7s. Here one such example is No. 47705 *Lothian*, which is standing at Glasgow Queen Street ready to head back to Edinburgh during 1980. (Author's Collection)

A glorious spring evening at Cogload Junction as No. 46055 heads away from the junction and down towards Taunton with a long rake of empty four-wheel China clay hood wagons from the potteries of Stoke-on-Trent to St Blazey. This working was known as the 'clayliner' and continues to operate in 2021. (Nigel Nicholls)

Until 1988 the vast majority of newspapers in England were printed in London or Manchester and were railed around the country overnight for delivery early the next morning. Here a battered No. 33031 waits at London Bridge station on 11 August 1987 with a combined newspaper and mail train for Kent. This is likely to be 1N01, the 03.10 for Maidstone West. Note the impressive single-span trussed-arch roof built by the London, Brighton & South Coast railway in the 1860s. Note also the incongruity of the mid-1970s footbridge, which provided access to the South Eastern platforms of the station. (Nic Joynson)

Having just passed beneath Frouds Lane bridge at Woolhampton HST set 253040 heads west along the classic Berks & Hants route on 27 August 1981 operating the 15.25 Paddington–Penzance service. (Tony Callaghan)

Thumper unit No. 1126 has just passed under Battledown Flyover, at Worting Junction, operating the 12.34 Basingstoke to Salisbury service on 31 March 1982. From fleets of 34 sets, these Class 205, or 3H, DEMU sets, which were known locally as 'Hampshire units', were allocated to Eastleigh and St Leonards depots. They would see out an incredible forty-seven years of service in total, with the final sets being withdrawn during December 2004. (Tony Callaghan)

Towards the end of their operational life with British Rail, the Class 55 Deltic saw use on the Trans-Pennine route to Liverpool, taking them well away from their normal sphere of operations. Unsurprisingly this was popular with enthusiasts, and on Tuesday 19 June 1979 No. 55015 *Tulyar* heads towards York station with the 17.05 Liverpool to Newcastle Trans-Pennine service, although there doesn't appear to be too many people travelling on board. (Nic Joynson Collection)

Saturday 29 October 1988 and No. 305402 leads the 10.40 London Liverpool Street to Shenfield past Stepney on the climb up Mile End bank towards Stratford. (Nic Joynson)

In unrefurbished condition No. 50004 stands at Paddington station while the driver is on the SPT (Signal Post Telephone) to the signalman at Old Oak Common to either remind them that he's standing at a red signal, or perhaps receive further instructions from the signalman on where the loco has to go. No. 50004 would go on to be named *St Vincent* in line with all other Class 50s, which were named after Royal Navy vessels. (Nigel Nicholls)

Consecutively sequenced Nos 40032 and 40033 are seen at Llandudno station in a nice burst of sunshine between the clouds. Twenty-six Class 40s were originally named after ships operated by Elder Dempster Lines, Cunard and Canadian Pacific steamships, as pre-West Coast Main Line electrification they would have hauled express services to Liverpool, the home port of these shipping companies. Changes from 1970 would see Class 40s removed from these services, and gradually their distinctive nameplates would be removed. For No. 40032, this was previously named *Empress of Canada*, and for No. 40033 this was previously named *Empress of England*. (Nigel Nicholls)

Captured here in West Wales, at Whitland station in the county of Dyfed, is a Class 47-hauled passenger service, most likely bound for London. The Class 120 DMU in the bay platform will be operating a service to Pembroke Dock. Note the headlight on the centre-front of the DMU between the cab windscreens, a requirement for operating over the Central Wales line. (Author's Collection)

Jacked-up, and with its bogies removed, is No. 33048 at Eastleigh depot on 11 December 1985, undergoing maintenance. Although a Hither Green-allocated machine, in reality it was irrelevant which depot a loco was allocated to if it required attention away from its home depot, as is obviously the case here. (Author)

Looking rather smart, while its new and clean, is this pair of white DMUs with an all-over blue unit at the rear, at Hest Bank early the mid-1970s operating a Leeds to Morecombe service. This white livery was applied to units undergoing refurbishment from 1974. Incredibly, this livery was applied to various units until 1984. (Ian Kay/Author's Collection)

Approaching Epsom station on 10 August 1982 is No. 508039, operating the 09.03 Dorking–Waterloo service. Primarily for suburban use, these Class 508 Electric Multiple Units (EMU) were built at BREL York and introduced during 1979 for use on British Rail's South Western and Southern divisions, with a fleet of forty-three four-car sets being built. The entire fleet was eventually transferred away from the Southern Region during the early 1980s for redeployment on Merseyside once the Class 455 had been fully commissioned. (Tony Callaghan)

Fine weather at Carlisle station on 13 April 1984 as No. 86213 *Lancashire Witch* has just dropped on to the 08.35 Stranraer–Euston service, having been brought in from Scotland with a Class 47. Through services between Stranraer and London finished on 14 May 1990, with the final overnight sleeper service. Daytime services had ceased by the end of the summer 1988 timetable. (Tony Callaghan)

Kirkham Abbey, between York and Malton, on the York to Scarborough route sees No. 40027 pass by working the 14.05 Scarborough to York on 17 August 1982. Formerly named *Parthia*, No. 40027 would be withdrawn from traffic some seven months later during March 1983, with final disposal coming during April 1984 at BREL Crewe. (Ian Kay/Author's Collection)

There was always something quite fascinating about standing at the end of the platform at Bristol Temple Meads station watching the comings and goings, and the adjacent depot – Bristol Bath Road – was a constant source of entertainment with movement either on or off the depot, or shunting around from one area to another. On 8 August 1986, Peak No. 45013 is shunting around the depot, much to the delight no doubt of those spectating from the platform. The somewhat bland blue livery has been brightened up with some additional white embellishments, making this particular locomotive easily recognisable. It would go on to receive the unofficial painted name *Wyvern* applied at Tinsley depot. (Author)

No. 03073 shunts the stock from the recently arrived 12.05 service from Kings Cross out of Hull Paragon on 12 April 1980. While the BG coach next to the locomotive is in 'ex-works' condition, the locomotive's external condition is the opposite. The bleached appearance is due to repeated runs through the carriage washing plant. British Rail washing plants used a product containing oxalic acid. Instructions for use were to apply it, let it dry and then rinse it off. If not washed off correctly then the chemicals attacked the paint finish, as seen here. (J.S Mattison/Nic Joynson Collection)

A lovely summer's day to enjoy the classic vantage point overlooking the pumping station at Crofton, on the Berks & Hants line, as a Hymek heads west towards Savernake on 6 August 1969 with a short ballast train in tow. British Rail's National Traction Plan of 1967 meant locomotive types, like the Hymek, were on borrowed time. After some ten years of service with British Rail, the 101 strong fleet were all withdrawn by 1975. Four examples entered into preservation. (Roger Smith Collection)

Classic Bournemouth line traction, 1960s style. The Class 432 4-REP unit, or **4-R**estaurant-**E**lectro-**P**neumatic, was a high-powered electric multiple unit (EMU) of 3,200 hp introduced for the Waterloo to Bournemouth line as a direct replacement for the outgoing steam traction. They would push or pull non-powered 4-TC sets to/from Bournemouth, with Class 33/1s taking the 4-TC sets to/from Weymouth. The line from Bournemouth to Weymouth was finally electrified from May 1988, some twenty-one years after the line to Bournemouth was electrified. With less than a year to go before their replacement by the then new Class 442 'Wessex Electric' units 4-REP No. 2003 approaches Totton on 16 August 1987 with the 09.51 Weymouth–Waterloo service with two 4-TC sets in tow. (Nic Joynson)

British Rail envisaged a new generation of diesel multiple unit in the 1970s, and plans were developed for two new diesel-electric units to be constructed at BREL Derby. One three-car and one four-car unit was built, and classified as Class 210. Evaluation of these units commenced during 1981. Here the four-car set, numbered as 210001, arrives at Langley operating the 09.52 Reading–Paddington service on 29 April 1983. By 1987 the two units had been withdrawn, but had proven their worth during their trials and would be the forerunner to other unit types that would introduced by British Rail. (Tony Callaghan)

A nice glint from the setting sun off the bodyside of No. 55012 *Crepello* at Hull station on 1 January 1979, prior to it working the 21.00 Hull to Doncaster service. To the left the cab of a Swindon-built Class 123 four-car Inter-City DMU can be seen. These units were originally built for the Western Region, but from the mid-1970s fell out of favour there and found continued use primarily on trans-Pennine services based at Hull Botanic Gardens depot until their final withdrawal in 1984. (JS Mattison/Nic Joynson Collection)

Summer in the South West during the late 1970s, and a day at Cogload Junction would yield all sorts of sights. On this day a pair of Class 25s, led by No. 25269, pass with a lengthy train of Mk1 coaches in tow along the Up Main from Taunton, destined for Bristol and the north. (Nigel Nicholls)

The wonderful St Pancras station in London, designed by William Barlow, and opened on 1 October 1868. Moving forward to 17 December 1986 and No. 317343 stands under the magnificent roof with the 20.20 St Pancras to Bedford service, the station clock showing there's one minute to go before departure. (Nic Joynson)

Once it was an everyday and ubiquitous scene on Britain's railways; the movement of coal. In 1987 the line through Knottingley in West Yorkshire enjoyed a constant procession of coal trains heading for the power stations at Drax and Eggborough. Here No. 56102, with a loaded MGR train, passes England Lane on 16 September 1987 with a train from Gascoigne Wood. Ferrybridge 'B' power station, which closed in 1992, dominates the scene. (Nic Joynson)

Always a hive of activity at Peak Forest, and Wednesday 8 July 1987 is no exception with two Class 47s in action, with No. 47109 closest to the camera. No. 47109 is backing down onto a loaded train of MSV wagons, which will leave later that morning for either Leeds or Bletchley. British Rail replaced these wagons with air-braked, four-wheeled wagons in 1988. (John Dedman)

A Class 31 approaches Kennett with BRT covered grain hoppers. Introduced in 1966 for Scottish Malt Distillers and Associated British Maltsters Limited, these 'Whiskey Covhops' wagons were coded PAA under TOPS. These wagons conveyed grain and malt between various terminals around the country. Pictured here was a flow of barley from various terminals in East Anglia for movement to north-east Scotland. Regular trains ceased in October 1992, with two brief trial flows in 1998. (Nigel Nicholls)

Winding through the Luxulyan Valley on 20 September 1986 with the 07.25 Manchester to Newquay is No. 50013 *Agincourt*. Scheduled loco-hauled services to the popular Cornish resort of Newquay would finally come to an end on Saturday 3 October 1987, the honour falling on No. 50026 *Indomitable*, which departed with 2C86 17.17 Newquay–Plymouth, having worked in with 1C36, the 11.10 Paddington–Newquay. (Barrie Renwick/Nic Joynson Collection)

The Railway Pictorial Publications Railtours (RPPR) promoted 'The Conway Consort' railtour from London Paddington on 7 October 1978, bringing Nos 24082 and 40113 to Blaenau Ffestiniog, which is where they are seen having just arrived. Tour participants are alighting onto the trackside for a photograph and to watch the loco's run-round their train. (Nic Joynson Collection)

A structure that made headline news on 8 February 1989 when the central parapet and two 73-foot arched spans were washed away following torrential rain in the area. The single track was left suspended above the River Ness and a further arched span of the 127-year-old viaduct was washed away with the torrent of water. A year before that dramatic event, and in glorious afternoon light, No. 37421 is captured passing over the Ness Viaduct on its approach to Inverness station on 16 February 1988 with the 12.02 Wick to Inverness service. The viaduct was rebuilt, and a new structure was opened on 9 May 1990 at a cost of £3.4 million, with an expected life span of 125 years. (Nic Joynson)

A bitterly cold winter's day at Reading on 15 January 1985 as a Class 101 diesel multiple unit idles away in Platform 7 between duties. (Author)

No. 33060 gets away from Salisbury, as seen from 'Skew Bridge', the A36 Wilton Road, with 1V77, the 15.15 Portsmouth Harbour–Cardiff Central, on Sunday 10 April 1988. This was only six weeks before loco-hauled services on the Portsmouth to Bristol/Cardiff route finished, Sprinter units taking over from Monday 16 May. (Nic Joynson)

A busy scene at Southampton Up Yard, also known as Bevois park, on 7 January 1988 as No. 47270 accelerates away with 6M93, the 14.55 Southampton to Willesden. The yard was busy enough to employ the services of a Class 08/09 shunter, which can be seen in the distance, and would trip between this yard and the one opposite known as Southampton Down Yard. (Nic Joynson)

A Class 08 stands at the head of some mail vans in Crewe station while Royal Mail staff load mail sacks into the vans. From the earliest days of the railway, Crewe was always a busy with mail traffic. Even as late as 1998, over twenty mail trains stopped at the station every twenty-four hours to load and unload traffic. The railway stopped carrying mail traffic in 2004, though in 2021 mail traffic is being carried once again. Nowadays, observers can no longer see mail trains at passenger stations, with surviving traffic running between dedicated Royal Mail terminals. (Author's Collection)

Looking very smart following its recent naming on 28 April 1986 is Eastfield's No. 47636 *Sir John de Graeme*, which is seen at Bristol Temple Meads on a TPO (Travelling Post Office) set. (Author's Collection)

The Railway Pictorial Publications Railtours (RPPR)-promoted 'The Welsh Wonder' railtour stands at Melksham on 25 November 1978. No. 25225 is leading No. 25157 and tour participants are free to get out and stretch their legs, even though the weather is cold and grey. The tour had originated at Paddington with this pair of Class 25s, which would continue on as far as Severn Tunnel Junction. Once in Wales, Nos 20044 and 20188 would take over to visit Blaenavon, Uskmouth and Bargoed. Finally. Nos 37180 and 37182 would takeover at Cardiff Central for the run back to Paddington via Gloucester. (Author's Collection)

The famous Great Western Railway works at Swindon is the location for No. 08702 undergoing overhaul on 27 February 1985. In its heyday the Great Western Railway employed some 14,000 people here. Through the latter part of the twentieth century workload declined and closure finally came on 27 March 1986, bringing to an end some 123 years of heritage and history. The site was redeveloped following closure and now includes a steam railway museum and retail outlets. (Author)

Along with the Deltics, the Westerns must surely rate as one of the most popular non-steam locomotive types to have graced Britain's railways. From an original build of seventy-four locomotives, introduced from 1961, seven would enter into preservation following withdrawal of the class by 1977. In the twilight of its operational life, No. 1051 *Western Ambassador* departs Reading station with a Paddington-bound service, withdrawal coming by early September 1976, and transfer to Swindon Works the following month for scrapping. (Author's Collection)

A classic Scottish location for railway photography was Princes Street Gardens in Edinburgh. On 17 August 1985, No. 27005, one of sixty-nine BRCW-built Class 27s, runs through the gardens with the 13.30 Dundee to Edinburgh service. (Nic Joynson Collection)

The Steam Locomotive Operators Association promoted 'Cumbrian Mountain Express' on 24 April 1984 featured A4 No. 60009 *Union of South Africa*, and employed Class 40 and 47 traction. In this photograph, No. 40015 is captured passing Armathwaite, heading north towards Carlisle. The Class 40 had worked the tour forward from Leeds, whereas the A4 would take the tour south back over the Settle & Carlisle. (Author's Collection)

With a set of Mk1 coaches in tow No. 81016 is captured near Tring on 26 August 1982 heading for London Euston. This locomotive type, originally designated AL1, was the first AC traction locomotive to be delivered to British Railways in late 1959, with a total build order of twenty-five locomotives. (John Dedman)

In the 1970s and 1980s British Rail were still using steam-era vehicles on a regular basis. In May 1980, the late Peter W. Gray captured No. 46017 at Cogload Junction, near Taunton, heading a southbound mail train. The consist was a variety of vintage vehicles, including many based on pre-nationalisation designs, all carrying variants of the rail blue livery. (Peter W. Gray/Nic Joynson Collection)

In June 1987 a Tyseley-based DMU is seen in the roofless steam shed at Machynlleth, hardly the perfect working environment for anyone expected to work on the outside of any train 'on shed'. (Author's Collection)

Sunday 30 December 1979 and Nos 73125 and 73110 pass Sway, near Brockenhurst, with 4W22, the 11:50 Poole–Waterloo empty van train. (John Dedman)

With single-line working in operation No. 37158 heads away from Bradford Junction 'wrong line' on 20 May 1990, working 2O87, the 07.45 Cardiff Central–Weymouth, with plenty of enthusiasts enjoying the loco, and the novelty, on board. In the distance is Bradford Junction, which had recently been remodelled and resignalled, the signal box closing on 18 March 1990 with control passing to Westbury Panel. (Steve McMullin)

Class 33s were the staple traction on the Bristol to Portsmouth services, having replaced Class 31s from the May 1980 timetable change. However, they still appeared on rare occasions, and on 20 March 1987, in amazing wintry conditions, No. 31428 heads towards Warminster working 1O42, the 13.05 Cardiff Central–Portsmouth Harbour. In the distance to the left the newly constructed bridge for the A350 Warminster bypass can be seen, although the new road either side of it has yet to be formed. (Steve McMullin)

On 8 September 1976, No. 1058 *Western Nobleman* stands at Yeovil Junction with 6B22, the 19.07 Westbury to Exeter Central cement train. The driver has surrendered the single line token from Yeovil Pen Mill to the signalman, and is about to continue on his way to Exeter. By January 1977 British Rail had withdrawn the locomotive and two months later it entered Swindon works for the final time. All but the seven locomotives saved by the preservation met their end at Swindon works. (Nic Joynson Collection)

Hard to imagine that Class 45s were regular visitors to Eastleigh, or the Southern Region, once upon a time. Here No. 45036 is passing the loco holding sidings opposite Eastleigh station on 12 June 1985. At this time 6O42, the 08.30 Severn Tunnel Junction–Eastleigh Yard 'Speedlink' trip, was a regular working for the class, and would return to South Wales on 6V83, the 16.10 Eastleigh Yard–Severn Tunnel Junction. No. 45036 had the distinction of being the final member of the class to carry this dot-matrix split headcode panel until withdrawal during May 1986. (Author)

Instantly recognisable by its silver-grey roof, this is a Stratford-allocated machine. No. 47010 hammers past Brookmans Park, along the East Coast main line, on 9 October 1979, heading south towards the capital. (John Dedman)

Stirling station featured a fine collection of semaphore signals into the twenty-first century. In September 1986, this pair of Class 101 DMUs, with set 101323 leading, waits to leave for Edinburgh or Glasgow. The early part of the twenty-first century has revolutionised the railway at Stirling. Today, modern overhead electric multiple units operate local services under colour-light signalling. (Roger Siviter/Nic Joynson Collection)

Running round their train load of china clay, Nos 37247 and 37301 pass the 1893-built GWR Type 5 signal box at Lostwithiel on 1 October 1984. The Class 37s may have long gone, replaced by more modern traction, but the fabulous signal box and its semaphore signals still remain in use into the 2020s. (Author's Collection)

A route popular amongst loco haulage enthusiasts was the Aberdeen to Inverness route, often referred to as 'over the top'. On 3 May 1989 at Elgin station is Inverness favourite No. 47550 *University of Dundee*, awaiting access onto the single line section to Keith while working 1A50, the 12.00 Inverness–Aberdeen. (Author)

Bubble-car T132 (No. 55032) arrives at Stourbridge Junction on 1 April 1989 with the shuttle service from Stourbridge Town. To the right is Stourbridge Junction box, a GWR Type 7B box opened in 1901. However, it would close on 24 August 2012 with control of the area passing to the West Midlands Signalling Centre at Saltley. The short half-mile branch line to Stourbridge Town, operated by London Midland, went over to regular operation by the Parry People Mover single car lightweight vehicles, designated as Class 139 by Network Rail, from June 2009. As for T132/No. 55032, it would enter departmental use as a sandite unit from December 1992 and be renumbered as ADB977842. However it would return to passenger use, including operation on the Cardiff Bay line during 2006. This Class 121 'bubble car' has also been modelled in OO gauge by various manufacturers, such as Dapol. (Author)

The British Rail Working Timetable shows headcode 'KA' is a working between the Southern Region's Central division and the Eastern, London Midland and Western Regions. It's the early 1970s in this lovely view at North Pole Junction as Crompton No. 6555 heads a loaded train of Simca vehicles. Under the creation of TOPS this locomotive would become No. 33037, and would remain in traffic until withdrawal until September 1987. (Roger Smith Collection)

The RCTS railtour 'Brighton Belle Commemorative' on 1 April 1972 departs from Newhaven Harbour formed of 5-BEL No. 3053. The tour started from London Waterloo and operated over numerous lines and branches around southern England, taking in locations like Portsmouth, Bognor Regis, Littlehampton, Eastbourne, Seaford, Newhaven and Brighton, before returning to London Victoria. The final Brighton Belle service ran on 30 April 1972 operated with these units, which were designated as Class 403 under TOPS. All three of these pre-war five-car units were then withdrawn from service, but all fifteen vehicles went onto private ownership. Some can still be seen in use with the British Pullman operated by Belmond. (Roger Smith Collection)

Newcastle station was synonymous with Class 03 shunters, and No. 03066, complete with the obligatory match-wagon, stands at the station on 3 April 1985. From a total build of 230 machines, incredibly fifty-six were preserved, including this particular locomotive, which is located at Barrow Hill engine shed. (Author)

On 6 April 1986 Class 50 No. 50049 *Defiance* worked 8Z10, the 07.45 Taunton Fairwater–Castle Cary Down Engineers Sidings with a tunnel inspection train for use the following Sunday at Grimstone Tunnel, between Maiden Newton and Dorchester West. The train is formed of Gantry YXW DM 721211 and tool van QPW DS 70159, which are pictured after arrival at Castle Cary. The loco would then run light engine to Yeovil Junction, where it would then work 7Z11, the 10.30 Yeovil Junction Tip–Exeter Riverside Yard spoil empties. (Steve McMullin)

On the Welsh Marches route at Abergavenny and No. 33029 arrives with a Crewe to Cardiff service. Driver training on Class 33s for Crewe drivers had commenced in 1981 and the class was soon established on the North & South route to replace the Class 25s. Their usage was relatively short lived, and they had themselves been replaced by Class 155 operating an hourly service from 1987 (although Class 37/4s were used due to the poor availability and temporary withdrawal of Class 155s), the Class 33s returning to their more traditional south of England duties. (Author's Collection)

Just two weeks away from withdrawal, on 2 August 1988, is No. 45128 *Centaur*, seen here stabled at Manchester Victoria on 16 July 1988 along with an inspection saloon. No. 45128 had the distinction of being the final Class 45 to be withdrawn, during March 1989, after a brief period of reinstatement. The proposal was to overhaul it for rail tour duties, although the decision was finally taken to scrap it, and final disposal followed during March 1992 at M.C. Metals in Glasgow. (Author)

Still a couple of years in traffic for No. 85023, before its withdrawal during April 1990. However, from an original fleet of forty locomotives only one would survive into preservation, with the rest being scrapped during the 1980s and 1990s. On 4 September 1987 No. 85023 stands at Birmingham New Street before departure with 1F12, the 11.39 Birmingham New Street–Liverpool Lime Street. (Author)

Having just passed through the 3-mile-long Woodhead Tunnel, No. 76037 leads No. 76034 through the closed Dunford Bridge station on the Woodhead line on 8 June 1977 working 6E36 Holyhead to Immingham. The station closed on 5 January 1970 to passenger services when the line lost its service between Manchester and Sheffield, despite objections and recommendations to keep the line open, and to close the Hope Valley line via Edale. (Author's Collection)

The same pair of Class 76s are seen continuing eastwards past Dunford Bridge signal box towards Penistone. The Woodhead line saw its final train just after 05.00 on 18 July 1981 following the passage of 6M10 Harwich to Trafford Park Speedlink working hauled by Nos 76006 and 76014, the line then being mothballed from Penistone to Hadfield. Removal of the overhead wires commenced immediately after closure, although full track lifting would not take place for a full five years. As part of an agreement between British Rail and the trade unions, a single line would remain, in the hope that the line may reopen. This reopening of course never came to fruition, and with one line lifted by 1983, the remaining single line would finally be recovered from 1986. (Author's Collection)

No. 55017 *The Durham Light Infantry* races along the East Coast main line at North Muskham to the north of Newark with a service for Kings Cross. When captured in the summer of 1981, No. 55017 had around six months of service remaining. The locomotive was withdrawn from service on 31 December 1981, along with four of the other survivors. The remaining three locomotives lasted until 2 January 1982. (Nic Joynson Collection)

A fine morning in the highlands of Scotland on 8 September 1989 as No. 47640 *University of Strathclyde* has just arrived at Pitlochry station working 1T20, the 10.15 Inverness–Glasgow Queen Street. (Author)

Having worked in on 2B21 11.04 Paignton–Exeter St Davids, No. 25048 has now run-round its train in the platform before setting off with its next working, the 2B26 14.16 to Paignton on 15 July 1980. Class 25s were based at Laira in Plymouth from October 1971 until November 1980. This particular locomotive arrived in May 1978 and, along with No. 25057, was the last Class 25 to leave Laira. The locomotive moved to Bescot and remained in service until 24 February 1986. (Nic Joynson Collection)

You can't get much further north than this. Standing at Wick at the head of 2H64, the 18.00 Wick–Inverness, is No. 37419 on 6 September 1987, prior to its 175-mile trip to the Highland capital. (Author)

Weymouth station looking in a rather sorry state, on a bright and pleasant day. As a Crompton stands in Platform 3, opposite in Platform 4 stands a Western Region DMU. The Brunel-designed station was demolished and replaced by a new station, which was officially opened on 3 July 1986. Electrification to Weymouth would also mean the end of Class 33 workings, with new electric services commencing on 16 May 1988. (Author's Collection)

The driver of Nos 03119 and 03141 is deep in conversation with another railman in the downside sidings at Pembrey & Burry Port in Carmarthenshire. The survival of Class 03s in West Wales was due to an idiosyncratic aspect of the Burry Port & Gwendraeth Valley line. Frequent flooding on the southern section of the line would interfere with the low-slung auxiliary equipment of the more common Class 08s, so in 1965 the Western Region modified two Class 03s locomotives with cut-down cabs and multiple working, with additional locomotives following. Much of the traffic on the line was coal for Carmarthen Bay power station at Burry Port. When the power station closed in 1984 the section of line that was prone to flooding was closed; the Class 03s were no longer needed and were replaced over the next few years by cut-down Class 08s. Both of the locomotives seen here have since been preserved. (Nic Joynson Collection)

Powering away from Bradford Junction on 21 January 1989 working 6C28, the 14.30 Westbury Up Yard–Lawrence Hill cement train, is No. 37431 *Sir Powys/County of Powys*. The train, formed of PCA type wagons, would have been tripped over from the nearby Westbury cement works at Heywood Road Junction to Westbury Yard, for onward movement. (Steve McMullin)

Withdrawn by British Rail during June 1988, but then passing into preservation, was No. 45041 *Royal Tank Regiment*. With only about ten months left in traffic before withdrawal, unnamed No. 45041 heads south through Sunderland Bridge, County Durham, on 14 September 1987 with a Tyne Yard to Ferryhill working formed of 16-ton vacuum-braked wagons. (Nic Joynson)

A view of Norwich station, as viewed from an arriving train late in 1977. Several Class 105 Cravens DMUs can be seen in this classic view, along with one Stratford's Class 47s, highlighted by the silver-grey roof that was to be a trademark of this east London depot, and of course the Class 03 shunter that for so many years was synonymous with Norwich. Note the yellow British Rail vans lined-up on the far right. (Author's Collection)

An all-blue two-car Class 105 Cravens DMU stands at Sudbury station during September 1983. The line here was once a through route to Shelford, near Cambridge, but British Railways truncated the route at Sudbury as part of the Beeching cuts. From March 1967 Sudbury became the terminus of an 11-mile branch from the Great Eastern mainline at Marks Tey. (Roger Siviter/ Nic Joynson Collection)

Passing the lofty March East Junction signal box, and into March station, on 4 July 1991 is Nos 20187 and 20040 working 6H46, the 15.17 Foxton–Whitemoor Yard. British Rail supplied Foxton Cement Works with imported coal from Kings Lynn Docks, which was used to fire the cement kilns. After unloading at Foxton, the train seen here was returning the empties to Whitemoor Yard for stabling. (Nic Joynson)

Pleasant weather at Arbroath station greets No. 26043 as it passes through on 11 August 1988 working 7L22, the 09.15 Dundee West–Dundee West via Montrose and Laurencekirk, conveying agricultural lime from Thrislington, County Durham, for Montrose. From an original fleet of forty-seven locomotives, an incredible thirteen Class 26s survive into preservation, including this example. (Author)

Ready for its 170-mile journey to South Wales is No. 37426 *Y Lein Fach/Vale of Rheidol* at the head of 1V18, 18.17 Manchester Piccadilly–Cardiff Central, on 6 June 1988. (Author)

Normally based at Inverness, snow blower ADB968500 has been brought south and is seen at Maidstone East on 17 January 1987 having just cleared the Up line of snow. It would then head to Lenham Heath on the Down line to assist with the clearance of snow, and recovery of No. 33061 trapped in the snow there. (Roger Smith)

Using traditional snowploughs, No. 33061 found itself trapped on 17 January 1987 in an impassable snowdrift near Forstal Road at Lenham Heath, between Lenham and Charing stations, on the Maidstone East to Ashford (Kent) line. (Roger Smith)

With the South East under a foot of snow, and more snow forecast, the 'big freeze', as ITN's *Coast to Coast* described it, was certainly making an impression with temperatures getting as low as -15°C overnight. This of course wasn't helping British Rail, and the depth of snow here is quite obvious on Saturday 17 January 1987, with what seems like an impossible task to free the trapped locomotive and its independent snowploughs. Services all over Kent were struggling in the wintry conditions, with Class 33s and Class 56s being used to haul electric service trains due to icy conductor rails and heavy snowfall. (Roger Smith)

It wouldn't be until dusk on Saturday 17 January 1987 that the Class 33 would be freed, but not without the heroic efforts of those on the ground clearing the snow. No. 47131 has been brought in to assist with the recovery. (Roger Smith)

On the approach to Woking on 2 April 1984 is classic Bournemouth line traction, the 3,200 hp Class 430 4-REP tractor unit. Here the 10.00 Bournemouth to Waterloo semi-fast service is powered by No. 3015, with a pair on non-powered 4-TC sets in tow. These units were replaced by the then-new Class 442 'Wessex Electrics' in May 1988. (Tony Callaghan)

A driver's-eye view on 26 November 1977 of oncoming No. 81021 near Stafford. In 1959 Associated Electrical Industries (AEI) delivered the first AL1 (later Class 81) locomotive to British Railways. The locomotives were originally used for testing and driver training on the first electrified section of the West Coast route: the Styal loop south of Manchester. (Roger Siviter/ Nic Joynson Collection)

Approaching Settle Junction on Saturday 16 August 1986, accompanied by gorgeous weather, is No. 47526 *Northumbria*. The Class 47 is working 1E33, 16.35 Carlisle–Hull, having travelled over the classic Settle & Carlisle (S&C) route. The line off to the left goes to Carnforth via Giggleswick, and anyone with a keen eye may spot the steam locomotive waiting at the signal to the far centre-left. This is S&D 7F No. 53809 with 'The West Yorkshire Limited' returning from Carnforth to St Pancras, which it will work as far as Leeds. (Roger Siviter/Nic Joynson Collection)

Accelerating away from Fratton is No. 33203, working a Brighton to Plymouth service. While not common on services such as this, the narrower Class 33/2 'slim Jim' variants did make occasional appearances, much to the delight of enthusiasts. (Pete Nurse)

A lovely scene at Crediton during March 1980 sees DMU sets P957 and P874 passing each other on services to or from Barnstaple. This former London & South Western double-track railway, which once formed part of a more extensive rail network in North Devon, was reduced to a single-line branch north of Crediton from 17 October 1971, and the remaining double-track section from Crediton to Cowley Bridge Junction was singled from December 1984. (Nic Joynson Collection)

In glorious weather on 19 June 1989 No. 20028 leads No. 20172 away from Crewe Basford Hall yard with loaded HAA hopper wagons. Both locomotives have the Kingfisher symbol associated with Thornaby depot painted on their bodysides. (Tony Callaghan)

On 23 October 1983 the 19.10 Gloucester to Paddington postal and parcels train waits at Reading worked by No. 50021 *Rodney* as its vans are loaded from the platform. (Tony Callaghan)

A trio of BR blue Class 31s stabled at Cardiff Canton on 6 July 1985 led by No. 31173, with No. 31113 in the centre and No. 31210 just visible under the water tower. This was on the occasion of the depots open day, which was held in connection with the GWR150 celebrations during 1985. Several Western Region depots were opened to the public, including Reading and Old Oak Common. (Author)

A class of locomotive in the twilight of its operational life, the Class 27. Built between 1961 and 1962, this fleet of sixty-nine locomotives would all be withdrawn by August 1987 – a relatively short lifespan, but typical of these early first generation locomotive types. On 2 April 1985 No. 27012 stands at Haymarket station with a Dundee-bound service. (Author)

It's fifteen minutes of fame for the humble Class 08 shunter No. 08815, which is seen hauling a replica of *Sans Pareil* at Rainhill on 24 May 1980 in connection with the 150th anniversary of the Rainhill Trials of 1829. (Author's Collection)

2-HAP No. 4305 leads a 4-VEP unit along the Down Fast at Raynes Park working a Waterloo to Portsmouth & Southsea stopper via Worplesdon. These two-car electric multiple units were ideal for branch line workings, although a journey of this length though might be pushing it for some passengers, especially if you're sat in the wrong coach as there was no gangway through to the other coach that had first class accommodation and a toilet. (Author's Collection)

At the top end of Redhill's Up platform stands all-over BR blue 2-EPB No. 5619, presumably about to form the front portion of a London-bound service, with a portion from somewhere like Brighton attaching to the rear. (Roger Smith Collection)

On 13 November 1981 No. 50022 *Anson* heads through West Byfleet heading the 11.10 Waterloo to Exeter service. Withdrawn from service during September 1988, this locomotive was finally disposed of during June 1989 at Vic Berry's of Leicester. However, from a fleet of fifty locomotives incredibly eighteen were to enter into preservation. (Tony Callaghan)

Now in preservation is No. 37264, currently based on the North Yorkshire Moors Railway. However, back on 12 June 1991 it could be seen passing Hawkeridge Junction leading 8A01, the 07.10 Gloucester New Yard–Westbury Up Yard formed of a rake of ZKV wagons. A new pre-assembled junction is laid out, and will then be dismantled and reassembled at Hawkeridge Junction over two weekend possessions. (Steve McMullin)

A busy moment at Carlisle on Sunday 22 April 1984 as No. 47593 *Galloway Princess* has arrived from Scotland, and is being uncoupled by the shunter. To the right No. 87015 *Howard of Effingham* and No. 47194 await their next turn of duty. (Roger Siviter/Nic Joynson Collection)

From an original fleet of eight, one of the Class 128 single parcels DMUs makes its way along the Up Main at Ruscombe on 6 February 1981. These units were operated by the Western and Midland regions of British Rail and were all withdrawn by 1990. None were preserved. (Tony Callaghan)

Seen with just ten days to go before closure on 25 April 1987, the GWR Type 8A signal box at Aller Junction. On 15 April 1987 No. 47538 passes at the head of 3S15, the 12.10 Penzance–Glasgow Salkeld Street mail train. Following the closure of the signal box, and resignalling, the physical junction was abolished, and would be known as Aller Divergence. (Steve McMullin)

A typical West Coast main line scene for many years as No. 87011 *The Black Prince* climbs towards Shap Wells during May 1978. British Rail Engineering Limited (BREL) built the Class 87s at Crewe Works and delivered them for service from 1973. As built, all thirty-six locomotives carried rail blue, with this livery lasting until sectorisation in the 1980s. (Author's Collection)

F&W Railtours 'The Chopper Topper' railtour on 31 August 1986 brought the incredibly rare visit of a pair of Class 20s to the far South West. After a failed first attempt on 8 June to get a pair of 20s into Penzance, due to the derailment of No. 37196 at Truro station, a more successful attempt took place in the August. However, from that original tour the train locos, Nos 20011 and 20054, did get to Long Rock depot at Penzance for fuel before heading back to Plymouth for the return working. In August, Nos 20094 and 20124 did make it into Penzance station, and became the first Class 20s at Penzance station. Here they are seen 'over the wall' prior to returning 'The Chopper Topper' back to Wolverhampton. (Author's Collection)

Quite an extraordinary scene on 20 March 1981 following the failure of the HST, which is hauled north by No. 40056 past Holme crossing box, south of Peterborough between Huntingdon and Fletton Junction on the East Coast main line. This illustrates how versatile British Rail locomotives and rolling stock were, something that would be eroded in years to come with the loss of such flexibility between certain types of new multiple units. (Nic Joynson Collection)

The humble Class 08 shunting locomotive, sometimes referred to by railwaymen as a '350', could once be found the length and breadth of the country, from small yards to large stations, and from back waters to branch lines. On 8 July 1985 this pair, Nos 08519 and 08724, are stabled up at the famous east London depot of Stratford. The depot closed in 2001, with the adjacent works closing a decade earlier. The site is now occupied by Stratford International station on the High Speed 1 route. (Author)

Stabled on what was the former steam shed at Wigan Springs Branch depot is No. 25225 at the head of a classic line-up of traction so typical of the north-west. This particular locomotive was withdrawn on 5 October 1980 after only seventeen years of operational service. (Author's Collection)

Passing Falsgrave signal box on Sunday 14 August 1983 is No. 47212, working 1L91, the 08.35 Wakefield Westgate–Scarborough, while a Class 08 shunter awaits to the left, most likely to shunt release the incoming stock. The impressive 120-lever London North Eastern signal box, which is Grade II listed, closed in September 2010. The signal gantry was carefully removed and is now in use at Grosmont on the North Yorkshire Moors Railway. (Roger Siviter/Nic Joynson Collection)

On the same fine day as the previous image, No. 40197 awaits departure with a return advertised excursion to Rhyl. In the adjacent platform, a Class 03 is shunting stock, while in the distance a Class 31, a Class 45 and a DMU are visible. With five sets of loco-hauled stock on view, Scarborough was clearly an impressive place to watch a variety of traction and workings back in the early 1980s. (Roger Siviter/Nic Joynson Collection)

In unrefurbished condition, and starting to look a bit shabby, No. 50011 sweeps round past Langstone Rock, near Dawlish Warren, with an eastbound service, most likely bound for Paddington. No. 50011 was assigned to Doncaster Works in February 1978 with accident damage and would not be released back into traffic until April 1979. In keeping with the rest of the class, which were named after Royal Navy Warships, No. 50011 would become *Centurion* on 17 August 1979. With the rundown of the class it became the first withdrawal in February 1987, and scrapped at Crewe Works in September 1992. (Nigel Nicholls)

Heading west across the Somerset Levels is plain BR blue No. 50049, seen here at Oath to the west of Langport, on the section of line between Castle Cary and Taunton. Due to reliability issues, British Rail would carry out a programme of refurbishment works on the fleet of fifty Class 50s between 1979 and 1984 at Doncaster Works. On 2 May 1978 No. 50049 would be named *Defiance*, in line with all other class members that were named after Royal Navy ships. (Nigel Nicholls)

The leaking steam heat from No. 37026 *Loch Awe* creates a nice bit of atmosphere at Arrochar & Tarbet station. On 1 April 1985 the Class 37 waits to pass an oncoming service occupying the single-line section to Ardlui while hauling the 08.30 Glasgow Queen Street to Oban service. (Author)

A location now transformed with overhead electrification and modern traction, but in March 1972 it still has a steam-age appearance as an unidentified Western approaches Newbury station heading west, while a DMU departs to the left going east towards Reading. (Roger Smith Collection)

Surrounded by the gorgeous Dorset landscape, No. 46050 departs from Maiden Newton heading towards Yeovil with a service from Weymouth. The Class 46s were all withdrawn by 1984, with two entering preservation. Rather famously, classmate No. 46009 (97401) may be remembered as being used in a crash test on 17 July 1984 at the Old Dalby test track, where it was automatically driven into a nuclear flask. The locomotive and its three Mk1 coaches were destroyed, but the flask remained intact. (Author's Collection)

Passing the somewhat dilapidated looking Mitre Bridge Junction signal box on 28 May 1981 is No. 31109 running light engine along Mitre Bridge curve, which leads to Willesden High Level Junction, and the North London Line. Incredibly the box survived into 1990 before closure on 20 May of that year, with control passing to Willesden Panel. (Tony Callaghan)

No. 47591 is seen at Basingstoke sporting a silver-grey roof, black headcode panel, and a large bodyside Eastfield Scottie dog. Here it stands at Basingstoke while working 1E63, the 10.38 Poole–Newcastle, on 22 October 1987. Coming up alongside on the left is No. 50010 *Monarch*, while a DEMU sits in the Reading bay over to the right. (Author)

Making its way along the former Gosport branch is No. 33007 working 6T50 from Eastleigh to Bedenham, formed of nine VEA vans. The branch was truncated at Bedenham in 1969 to continue to serve the Royal Naval Armaments Depot, with final closure occuring in 1991. (Pete Nurse)

No. 86205 *City of Lancaster* hurries through Bushey on 7 April 1983 with a service from London Euston. (John Dedman)

Ashton Gate engineers sidings in Bristol on 4 March 1988 and No. 47558 *Mayflower* shunts a tunnel inspection train prior to departure as 9Z5, the 1 11.30 Ashton Gate–Bristol East Depot. When the trains were required for such work they would be tripped to Bristol East Depot for remarshalling with other wagons. Brunel's Clifton Suspension Bridge can be seen in the distance, and the Portishead branch is to the left, which travels beneath it alongside the banks of the River Avon. (Steve McMullin)

A great overview of the east end of Edinburgh Waverley station from above Calton Tunnel. With plenty of platform-end railway enthusiasts there to watch and record its arrival, a Class 55 Deltic has just made a typically smoky exit from the tunnel and into the station. There's plenty of other interest as well for the enthusiasts to enjoy, including a Class 27 and 40 in the bay platform, two Class 08 shunting locos, and a Class 47-hauled passenger train in Platform 10. (Author's Collection)

Under a very moody sky No. 86214 *Sans Pareil* runs into Crewe during July 1981. This was a year full of event, such as 'Yorkshire Ripper' Peter Sutcliffe being arrested by police; Ronald Reagan being sworn in as the fortieth President of the United States; Bucks Fizz winning the Eurovision Song Contest with *Making Your Mind Up*; riots in Brixton and Toxteth; and Prince Charles marrying Lady Diana Spencer. (Author's Collection)

In unfamiliar territory on 13 April 1985 at Dover Western Docks station stands No. 50050 *Fearless*, having arrived with Hertfordshire Railtours 'The Dungeness Pebbledasher'. The railtour, which had started from Reading, would visit towns in the south-east such as Dover, Folkestone Harbour, Dungeness and Eastbourne, The tour featured Class 50 traction, but also utilised more familiar Southern Region Class 33 and 73 traction as well. Immediately to the right of the Class 50 is the First World War memorial created in remembrance of the 556 South Eastern & Chatham Railway employees who had fallen during the First World War. Formerly known as Dover Marine, this listed station was to close completely on 19 November 1994. (Author's Collection)

It is late afternoon on Saturday 28 February 1987 as a Class 105 DMU, with No. 54429 leading, generates a characteristic blue haze as it departs from Cambridge for the long trudge northwards to Doncaster via Peterborough. In February 1987 the overhead wires were newly installed and energised for operations between Cambridge and Bishops Stortford. Yet most through express trains between London, Cambridge and King Lynn remained diesel locomotive operated until May 1987. When the photograph was taken, Cambridge was the limit of electrification, with the project to electrify to Ely and King Lynn not approved until 1989. (Nic Joynson)

Presumably the Class 47 was in need of some assistance as No. 31307 leads No. 31170 away from Dawlish on 20 September 1979. With a dead 117-ton loco and twelve coaches in tow, they were probably making quite a racket as they head into Kennaway Tunnel. (Nic Joynson Collection)

On a January night in 1984, No. 27004 sits in the carriage sidings on the west side of Carlisle station. Class 27s were frequent visitors to Carlisle, typically working passenger services from Glasgow via Dumfries up until the summer of 1985. However, they could also be seen in the area on freight and parcels traffic right up until full withdrawal of the class in 1987. (Roger Siviter/ Nic Joynson Collection)

With the train crew apparently enjoying a joke, No. 08905 shunts two Seacow ballast hoppers at Acton Canal Wharf on 17 January 1990. The single surviving cooling tower from the defunct Acton Lane power station dominates the background. The Midland Railway-constructed Acton Canal Wharf signal box in 1895 controls the junction between the Dudding Hill Line, which connects Cricklewood and Acton. The line to Cricklewood continues into the distance, whereas the Class 08 is on a line that connects to the West Coast Main Line. (Nic Joynson)

On Tuesday 3 February 1981, the UK prime minister was Margaret Thatcher, the US President was Ronald Reagan, and head of the Catholic Church was Pope John Paul II. Meanwhile in Surrey, the 13.46 Waterloo to Bournemouth semi-fast service approaches Byfleet & New Haw formed of a typical 8-TC and 4-REP set, led by 4-TC 403. (Tony Callaghan)

One of the ten original Class 44 Peaks, No. 44009 *Snowdon* slows for its Chesterfield stop while working the 'Farewell Class 44' railtour on 21 January 1978. This British Rail-organised tour from Nottingham took No. 44009 across the Pennines via Beighton, Tinsley, Wath and Penistone. At Crewe, No. 44008 *Penyghent* replaced No. 44009 and worked the train back to Nottingham. Unfortunately the tour participants were in for a cold journey: the steam heating boilers on both locomotives were inoperable. A Class 24 was added to the train from Crewe to Chester to briefly defrost the passengers. As it happened, this farewell tour was a little premature: the Class 44s continued to work coal trains around Toton until November 1980. Derby Works scrapped No. 44009 in July 1980. (Nic Joynson Collection)

A period of transition on the Bournemouth line, before the introduction of the then-new Class 442 'Wessex Electrics'. Traction motors from the existing Class 430 4-REP units were reused in the new units. Ahead of the arrival of the new units, the phased withdrawal of the 4-REP units for removal of their traction motors was necessary. Network SouthEast's temporary solution was to use Class 73s operating in push-pull mode. Here large-logo No. 73139 passes Lyndhurst Road station on 15 August 1987 working the 11.00 Bournemouth–Waterloo semi-fast service. Lyndhurst Road was renamed Ashurst (New Forest) from 24 September 1995. (Nic Joynson)

In crisp winter conditions, an English Electric-powered DEMU, No. 204004, powers away from Southampton on 31 January 1987 while working a Portsmouth Harbour to Salisbury 'all stations' service. An everyday scene at the time, but even the mundanity of the traction disguises an example of the various twists and turns of Southern Region traction. The centre cars of the Class 204 were former EMU driving trailers, reformed in 1986 after the former 'tadpole' DEMUs were disbanded. The cab window of the former driving car is visible at the front of the second coach as well as the disused multiple unit jumper cables. (Nic Joynson)

A very grey and wintry scene at the west end of Reading station on Tuesday 15 January 1985 as No. 50002 *Superb* runs-round its train before heading off towards Oxford. (Author)

Tucked around the back of Old Oak Common depot on 27 May 1986 is former Scottish Region Class 06 No. 06003, now renumbered as 97804. The diminutive 0-4-0 shunting locomotive had been assigned to departmental use at Reading signal works following its withdrawal during 1981, where it spent a relatively short spell, final withdrawal coming during 1984. From an original fleet of thirty-five locomotives introduced in 1958 this would become the only member of the class to enter into preservation. (Author)

No. 33020 leads No. 33030 outside Westbury's TOPS office as they run around their train on 11 July 1988. They had just arrived with 7O70, the 16.30 Meldon Quarry–Eastleigh. Once the locomotives are on the other end of their train they will continue on to Eastleigh at the booked time of 21.15. (Steve McMullin)

Making a fine sight, No. 40058 makes its way through Doncaster with 6S93, the 14.25 Parkeston–Bathgate, formed primarily with loaded cars. (Author's Collection)

Along the sea wall at Sprey Point, between Dawlish and Teignmouth, is No. 45048 *The Royal Marines* heading west towards Teignmouth during the summer of 1983. Classes 45 and 46 were daily visitors to Devon and Cornwall, with some Class 46s being allocated to Laira depot at Plymouth. All Class 46s were withdrawn by the end of 1984. From October 1985 the remaining Class 45s still in traffic were banned west of Bristol following an incident involving a member of the class at Weston-Super-Mare. Of course, this didn't prevent occasional members slipping through the net and continuing to make appearances beyond Bristol. (Nic Joynson Collection)

Inside the maintenance shed at Toton TMD on 13 June 1992 is No. 08607, which is jacked-up with its back wheel set removed. By this time rail blue could still be found on some Class 08 shunters, but was almost abolished on main line locomotives. (Author's Collection)

A fine morning at Milley Bridge near Waltham St Lawrence, between Twyford and Maidenhead, as No. 50036 *Victorious* hurries towards the capital with the 08.55 Bristol Temple Meads to Paddington service on 28 November 1981. (Tony Callaghan)

A pair of Class 121 single-car diesel multiple units stand at Exeter St Davids on 10 August 1991 with a service bound for Exmouth. These came from a fleet of twenty-six coaches that made up the Class 121, and were introduced during 1960 for use on British Railways' Western Region. These single-car diesel units, referred to as 'bubble cars', were the obvious choice for light branch line operations. (Author)

The unique No. 47901 prepares to depart from Westbury on 11 June 1987 with a loaded stone train formed of ARC-branded four-wheel PGA wagons. Following accident damage at Peterborough in September 1974 when numbered 47046, the locomotive was chosen as a test bed for the Class 56 programme and fitted with a Ruston-Paxman engine, and renumbered as 47601. With the Class 58 programme it was again used as a test bed and renumbered to 47901. This unique Class 47 was scrapped by February 1992. (John Dedman)

A spruced-up Class 105 Cravens DMU can be found at Stratford depot on 8 July 1985 alongside another classmate. The unit, formed of vehicles 53359 and 54122, had been specially bulled-up for Stratford open day and was chosen to operate the final shuttle service on Friday 5 July 1985 between Stratford and Tottenham Hale, with a commemorative headboard reading 'Farewell Stratford–Lea Bridge–Tottenham Hale'. With no weekend service Lea Bridge station closed after the final train departed, the official closure date being listed as 8 July 1985. However, a change in fortunes for this once neglected station and route saw Lea Bridge reopened on Sunday 15 May 2016, and with a projected 350,000 passengers by 2031 things are finally looking up. (Author)

The Class 26, or the BRCW Type 2, was introduced in 1958 and totalled forty-seven locomotives. A line-up of three Class 26s are seen here at Inverness depot, with a very spruce No. 26024 at the head. A large portion of the class were allocated to Inverness and could be found on a variety of traffic on all routes out of the Highland capital. The remainder of the class were allocated to Edinburgh's Haymarket depot. By May 1987 the fleet had been transferred and centralised to Glasgow's Eastfield depot, and by October 1993 the entire class had been withdrawn from service. (Author's Collection)

Crewe was the birthplace of the majority of the highly popular Western locomotives Introduced between 1961 and 1964 a total of seventy-four locomotives were built, thirty at Swindon Works and forty-four at Crewe Works. In the run-up to the final withdrawal of the class a frenzy of railtours were organised, and on 29 January 1977 Swindon-built No. D1023 *Western Fusilier* is seen passing Crewe North signal box with the 'Western Memorial' tour that had originated at Paddington and was destined for Chester. Following withdrawal the locomotive entered preservation as part of the national collection at York National Railway Museum. (Nic Joynson Collection)

Just an everyday scene on 22 May 1986 at Liverpool Lime Street station. To the left in the centre siding is No. 25279, with No. 08532 tucked-in behind, while alongside a DMU sits in Platform 3 between duties. To the right is 31450, most likely having arrived on a service from Hull or Cleethorpes. (Author)

A beautiful Christmas card setting as 4-VEP 7759 departs from Lyndhurst Road station on Sunday 10 February 1985. With headcode '97' up front, this indicates this is a Waterloo to Lymington Pier service. (Malcolm S. Trigg/Author's Collection)

Crossing Canute Road in Southampton on 29 April 1983 is No. 73136 with the QE2 Boat Train from London Waterloo. The loco displays the correct headcode '95', indicating a train from Waterloo to Southampton Eastern Docks. (John Dedman)

A platform packed with smartly dressed commuters, all undoubtedly heading into the capital, prepare to board Class 415 4-EPB unit No. 5308 at Purley working a Brighton to London Victoria semi-fast service. (Roger Smith Collection)

This nocturnal scene at London's Euston station during 1984 sees No. 85023 ready to depart, possibly with an empty stock working. (Author's Collection)

The Settle & Carlisle in all its glory, with Wild Boar Fell dominating the skyline. At 1,167 feet above sea level Ais Gill is the summit on the line between Garsdale and Kirkby Stephen. On 26 April 1982, approaching the summit is No.40080 with a train of Speedlink vans, possibly from Warcop. (Tony Callaghan)

A scene full of character, with
wooden post semaphore signals
and an elegant, though somewhat
shabby, station. On 27 April
1982 a Class 108 DMU is seen
at Hellifield station operating the
15.35 Leeds to Morecambe service
in some fine springtime weather.
(Tony Callaghan)

DEMU No. 205006 crosses the
main road through the centre of
Uckfield on 25 September 1987
as it departs with the 11.42 to
London Victoria. Uckfield was once
on a through route to Lewes but
after May 1969 Uckfield became a
terminus station. In 1990, Network
SouthEast relocated the station to
the ground immediately in front
of the photograph, allowing the
removal of the congested level
crossing and closure of the signal
box. (Nic Joynson)

Coming off the former London &
South Western route from Crediton,
at Cowley Bridge Junction near
Exeter, is No. 33055 leading
No. 33027 *Earl Mountbatten of
Burma* on 20 June 1988 working
7O70, 16.30 Meldon Quarry–
Eastleigh PAD formed of loaded
Seacow ballast wagons. The
locomotives will run-round their
train at nearby Exeter Riverside
Yard before continuing on their
way via Taunton and Westbury.
(Steve McMullin)

Deltic No. 55015 *Tulyar* hammers north at Sandy with a service out of Kings Cross. Tulyar was an Irish-bred, British-trained,thoroughbred racehorse, with six major wins to his name. The locomotive named in his honour was one of six, out of a fleet of twenty-two, to enter into preservation following full class withdrawal at the start of 1982. (Nigel Nicholls)

Grangemouth depot near Falkirk with a trio of Class 27s and 37s on shed. The depot closed during 1992 and was redeveloped as a rail-served W.H. Malcolm Ltd depot. (Pete Nurse)

Another trainload of coal worked by large-logo-liveried No. 56103 passes through Mexborough, most likely originating from nearby Wath. The locomotive still looks relatively new, having been introduced new into traffic from 1982. Although there were mass withdrawals of the 135-strong Class 56 fleet in the late 1990s and early 2000s, this one is actually still in service into the 2020s. (Author's Collection)

A glorious sunrise at Newton Meadows, near Bath, on 15 January 1988, with the morning sun glinting beautifully off the side of No. 33040 and its train while passing with 2C16, the 06.55 Yeovil Pen Mill–Bristol Temple Meads. (Steve McMullin)

A slight twist on the all-over blue livery of the Class 31 was the addition of a white stripe midway along the bodyside, primarily applied by Finsbury Park and Old Oak Common depots. On the evening of 2 April 1985, Finsbury Park-allocated No. 31404 stands at Newcastle with a van train. (Author)

The afternoon light catches these two shunting locomotives rather nicely at Eastleigh depot. To the left is No. 08847, while to the right is No. 09001. Visually there is no difference between the two classes, however the Class 09 has a top speed of 27 mph in comparison to the Class 08's maximum speed of 20 mph. A total of twenty-six Class 09s were introduced, and could be found in use throughout the Southern Region. (Author)

On their home depot of Tinsley, in Sheffield, on Saturday 16 August 1987, this trio of Class 45s were stabled up for the weekend. In the twilight of their operational life are No. 45049 *The Staffordshire Regiment (The Prince of Wales's Own)*, with No. 45012 *Wyvern II* in the centre, and furthest from the camera is No. 45046 *Royal Fusilier*. Two months later, No. 45049 would be withdrawn from service during October 1987. No. 45012 would soldier on a little longer until withdrawal during July 1988, and the following month, August 1988, would see No. 45046 taken out of traffic. All three locomotives would be scrapped at MC Metals in Glasgow. (Author)

One of the final trains to be manufactured for British Rail in blue and grey livery, the Class 455 Electric Multiple Unit. Built for the Southern Region's Central and South Western divisions, the first of these new trains entered service during March 1983. Here No. 455708 arrives at Clapham Junction with a Waterloo to Guildford service. (Author's Collection)

With British Rail sectorisation just around the corner, and brand-new Class 58 locomotives coming off the production line in a new Railfreight grey livery, it was perhaps surprising to see locomotives and stock still being turned out in Monastral blue. On 10 March 1985, looking immaculate, are Nos 47372 and 20084 outside Crewe Works following overhaul. By comparison, Nos 58026–58029 were about to come off the BREL Doncaster production line. Rail blue was entering its twilight zone. (Author's Collection)

The first of the production Pacers, No. 141001 is stabled outside of the Railway Technical Centre at Derby in the summer of 1984. These were the first new production DMUs in the UK for more than twenty years and were built at BREL Derby using a Leyland National bus body. British Rail provided the four-wheel underframe and traction equipment. The first six Class 141s were also the last diesel-powered trains to be delivered in rail blue, or almost rail blue! British Leyland painted the bodies in a slightly darker blue, known as Barrow Corporation blue, which BL had used on a recent batch of buses. (Nic Joynson Collection)

By 1983 the era of rail blue was in sight, with the introduction of British Rail's brand-new Class 58 heavy freight locomotive, which was painted in an attractive Railfreight grey livery. Here brand-new No. 58002 is seen on Doncaster Works awaiting acceptance into traffic. (Dave Ware/Author's Collection)